Volcanoes

Written by
Jill Atkins

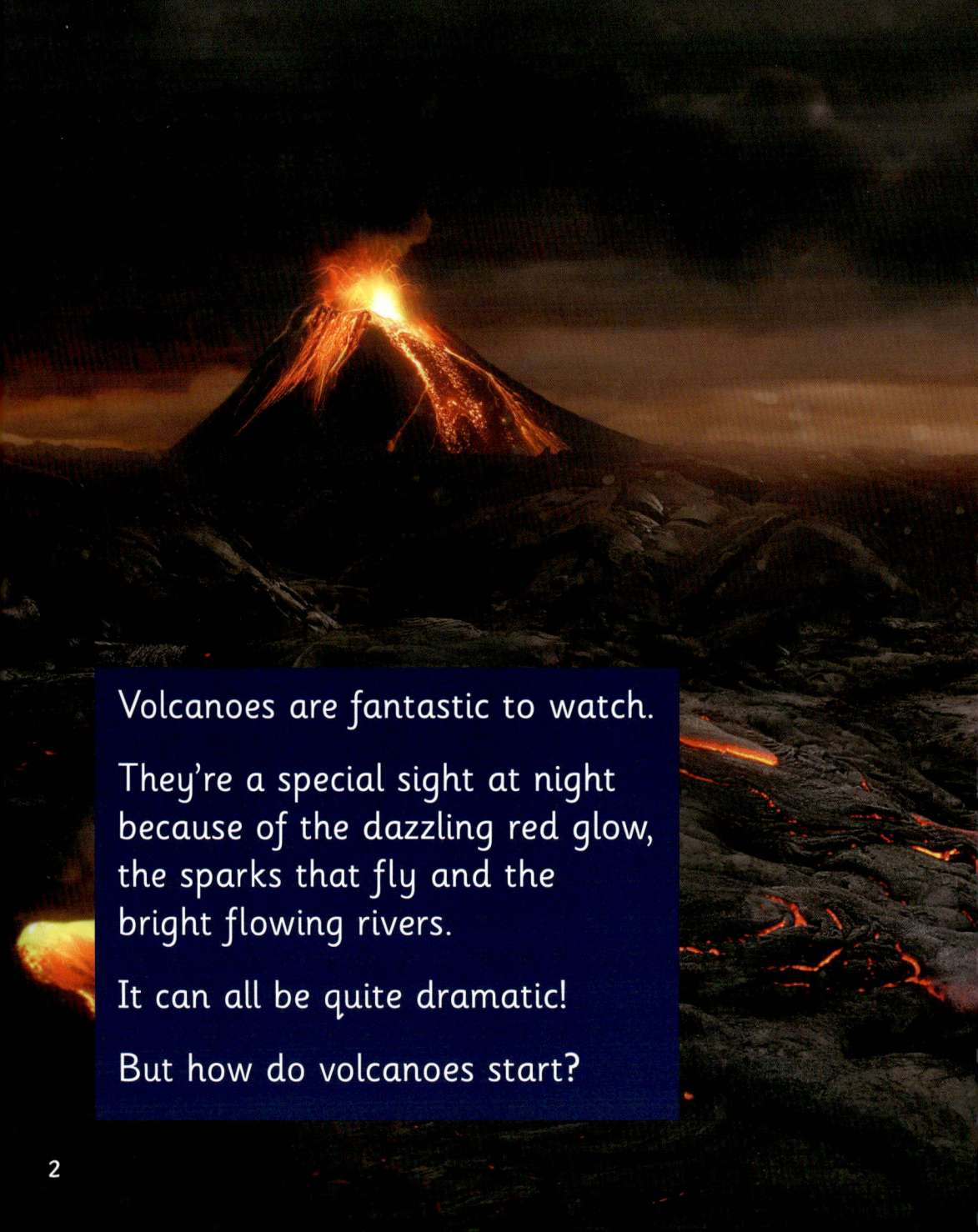

Volcanoes are fantastic to watch.

They're a special sight at night because of the dazzling red glow, the sparks that fly and the bright flowing rivers.

It can all be quite dramatic!

But how do volcanoes start?

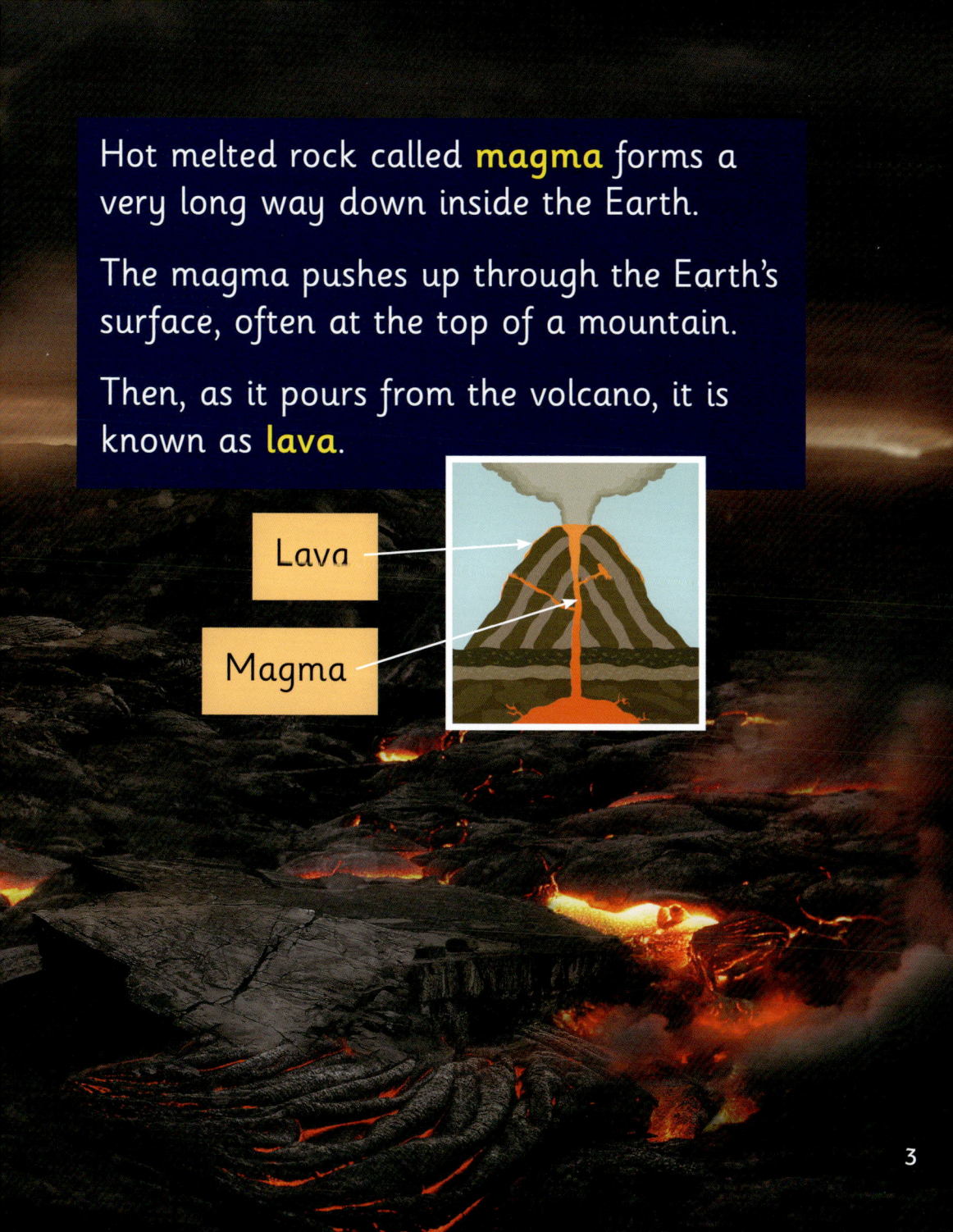

Hot melted rock called **magma** forms a very long way down inside the Earth.

The magma pushes up through the Earth's surface, often at the top of a mountain.

Then, as it pours from the volcano, it is known as **lava**.

Lava

Magma

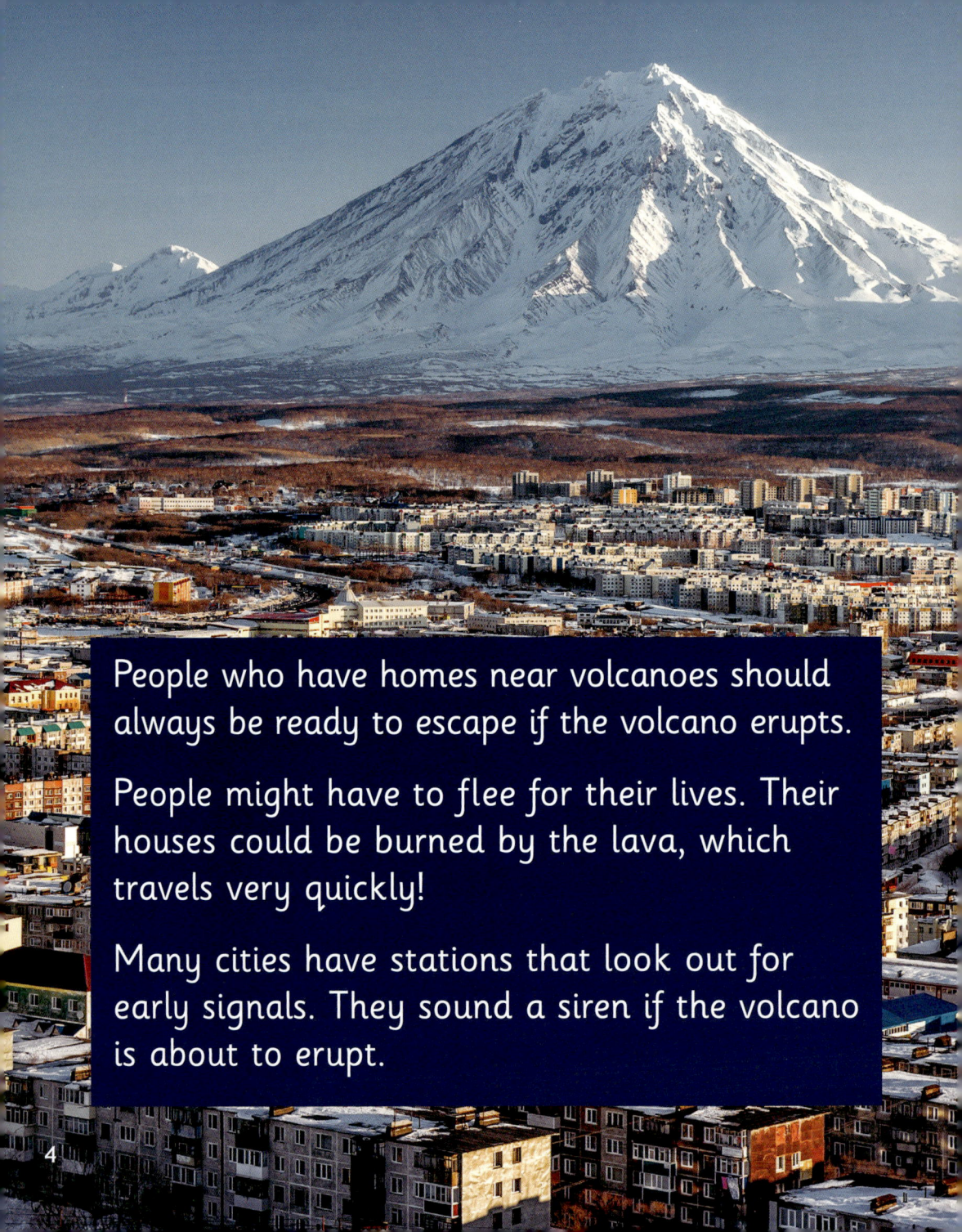

People who have homes near volcanoes should always be ready to escape if the volcano erupts.

People might have to flee for their lives. Their houses could be burned by the lava, which travels very quickly!

Many cities have stations that look out for early signals. They sound a siren if the volcano is about to erupt.

As lava cools, it hardens into rock or turns into black soil, which is good for growing crops.

Sometimes there is a colossal explosion. This can send showers of molten rock and gas into the air.

Some strong volcanic eruptions throw up vast clouds, made of the tiniest bits of magma, into the air. This is called volcanic dust, or ash.

The clouds are sometimes blown a long way, so the ash coats the land for miles around the volcano.

In Roman times, there was a huge eruption from this volcano and a whole city was completely covered by the ash that blew from the mountain.

The city was discovered hundreds of years later.

When volcanoes are not erupting, they are called **dormant** or **extinct**.

Dormant volcanoes are "asleep" and have not erupted for a very long time, but there is always a chance that they might wake up and erupt one day.

Extinct volcanoes are not expected to erupt ever again.

This volcano in Japan is dormant

When a volcanic eruption has ended, there is often a crater left at the top of the mountain.

Look at the lake in this crater.

People can sometimes climb up the side of a volcanic mountain. They can stand on the top and look down into the crater — but first they should make sure it won't erupt!

People who study volcanoes are called **volcanologists**. They even go down into the crater of a volcano to do experiments and learn about volcanoes.

Sometimes they need to wear masks to protect them from gases coming from the volcano.

You might wonder if there are clues to tell you that a volcano is about to erupt.

Yes, there are a few warning signs. There could be plumes of smoke that rise from the ground, or there might be a few small earthquakes.

Some volcanic eruptions take place under the sea. When this happens, a new land is sometimes formed.

This volcanic mountain in the sea is in Italy.

Do you think volcanoes are interesting? Perhaps one day you will become a volcanologist!

Many volcanoes are in what we call **The Ring of Fire**, around the Pacific. This stretches down the coast of North and South America on one side and Japan and down to New Zealand on the other side.

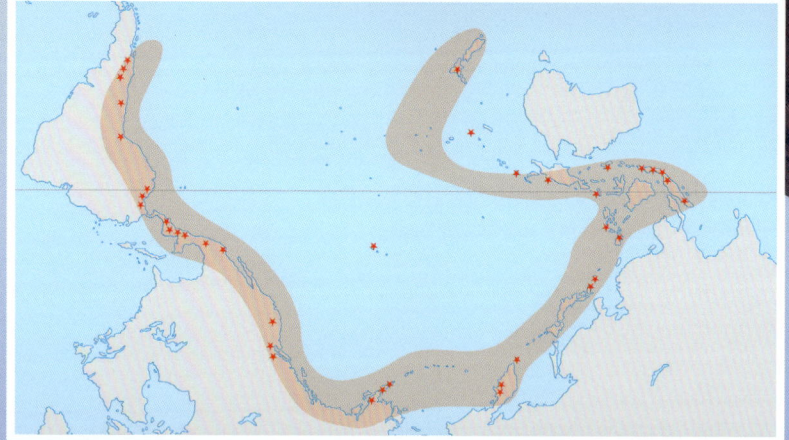